HOUGHTON MIFFLIN

Reading

A Legacy of Literacy

One Land, Many Trails

HOUGHTON MIFFLIN   BOSTON • MORRIS PLAINS, NJ

California • Colorado • Georgia • Illinois • New Jersey • Texas

Design, Art Management and Page Production: Kirchoff/Wohlberg, Inc.

ILLUSTRATION CREDITS
4-25 Craig Spearing. **26-29, 31-40, 42-47** Cedric Lucas. **48-69** Beth Peck.
70-71, 73, 75-77, 79-83, 85-91 José Miralles.

Printed in U.S.A.

ISBN: 0-618-04411-6

6789-VH-05 04 03 02

One Land, Many Trails

Contents

Shell-Flower

by Rhonda Rodriguez
illustrated by Craig Spearing

Strategy Focus

Can Shell-Flower overcome her fear of the strangers in her land? As you read, try to **predict** how her feelings might change.

They came with guns that made lightning and sounded like thunder. They came with hair on their white faces. The white men arrived in Paiute (PIE-yoot) country, and they came like great roaring lions.

Shell-Flower was still a very little girl when the news arrived for the first time: White men were nearby.

Shell-Flower's grandfather was the chief of all the Paiute people. When he heard the news, he jumped up and clapped his hands. "My white brothers!" he cried. "They have finally come!"

Grandfather had heard of the white people from far away. He called them his long-lost brothers. He wanted to meet them. Grandfather went to greet the strangers.

Grandfather took a band of men with him. He came to the white men's camp, but they would not meet with him. They turned him away.

Still, Grandfather was filled with hope. He had seen his white brothers for the first time. He returned to Shell-Flower's village and told this story.

In the beginning of the world, there were four children. There was one dark boy, one light boy, one dark girl, and one light girl.

When the children were young, they got along well. But as they grew older, they argued. This made their mother and father sad.

"Why do you argue? You are family," the father said.

The children were ashamed. But there was no peace among them. The parents could bear it no longer.

"If you cannot be good to each other, then you must remain apart," the father said. "Go across the great ocean. Stay out of each other's lives."

The dark girl and boy left together. They went to one side of the ocean. They were the first people of our nation.

The light boy and girl went to the other side of the ocean. They became the white people's nation.

We have waited all this time for someone to come to us from the white nation, to bring us together again.

Years passed. Grandfather finally met his white brothers. He traveled to their cities in California. He grew to admire and even love his white brothers. Every spring he returned to the Paiute homeland. He told Shell-Flower and her people about the wonders of the white brothers.

"They build houses that can travel," Grandfather said. "Some of their houses travel over the ocean, blown by the wind. They are faster than our horses! Other houses travel across the land on wheels."

One of the white brothers, John Fremont, had given Grandfather a paper. "When we show this to our lost brothers and sisters, it will tell them who we are," Grandfather said. "No harm will come to us when they see it."

For a time, Shell-Flower also longed to meet the white people.

Then came the awful spring when the Paiutes heard terrible news of the white man. Grandfather was away in California, and Shell-Flower's father was now Chief of the Paiutes. Shell-Flower's father was not as trusting of the white brothers. "They look like owls," he said.

Stories came from other tribes that the white brothers were killing many native people. The adults told Shell-Flower of horrible things that the white brothers were doing.

Shell-Flower was terrified. "How could Grandfather admire such men?" she wondered.

Shell-Flower's father sent his people into the mountains to hide for the winter.

One day, an alarm passed through Shell-Flower's camp: "The white people are coming!" Everyone began to run.

Shell-Flower's baby sister was strapped on Mother's back. Mother grabbed Shell-Flower's hand. They ran through the camp. Shell-Flower was so afraid, her legs could not keep up. Shell-Flower's aunt also had a small girl who could not run fast enough.

"We must hide our girls!" cried Shell-Flower's aunt.

The two mothers dug holes into the earth. They lowered each girl into a hole up to her neck. They filled the holes with soft soil. They placed sage bushes over the girls' faces to protect them from the sun. "Do not make a sound," said Shell-Flower's mother. "The earth will keep you safe."

Then Mother and Aunt ran off.

Shell-Flower and her cousin stayed quiet. They did not even whisper to each other. Fear pounded inside them. What if the white people found them?

For hours, Shell-Flower waited for something terrible to happen. Day turned to night.

Then, in the darkness, Shell-Flower heard low voices. Footsteps came close. Shell-Flower's throat closed in terror. "Here. Here they are," said a voice. It was her mother and father! The two children were lifted out of their holes. With Father's arms around her, Shell-Flower slowly stopped trembling.

Shell-Flower would never forget that terrible day. It made her fear the white brothers that Grandfather so loved.

Later that year, other white men destroyed the Paiutes' food and winter supplies. Shell-Flower's father gathered his people and told of a terrible dream he had had. In it, the land of the Paiute was overrun by the white men. Many Paiutes were killed. "To avoid bloodshed, we must all go to hide in the mountains. When my father returns, he will tell us what to do," Shell-Flower's father told his people.

But when Grandfather returned, he did not share his son's fear. He now wanted Shell-Flower and her family to come with him to California. He would bring Shell-Flower to meet his white brothers.

The journey to California began in the late fall. Grandfather led many Paiute families. Shell-Flower traveled with her mother, her brothers, and her sisters. Her father remained in the homeland with the rest of the Paiute people.

Shell-Flower rode behind one of her brothers. They traveled along a river and camped each night. On the third day, some men who had gone ahead came back to the group. "We have seen our white brothers' houses up ahead," they reported.

"Stop here," Grandfather told the group. "I will go to meet them."

Grandfather returned with gifts of food from his white brothers. "I showed them my paper. As long as I have it, we are safe," he said. "We will camp near the white brothers tonight."

Shell-Flower remembered the time she had been buried. This time, she hid under her brother's fur robe. As the horses began to move ahead, she cried against his back.

"Please, let's camp somewhere else tonight," said Shell-Flower's mother. "My daughter is too frightened."

Grandfather agreed. As the group rode by the white men's houses, Shell-Flower kept her head under the robe. She did not want to see.

But soon Shell-Flower finally saw the white strangers for the first time. Grandfather brought two white men back to meet the group of travelers. The men smiled at Shell-Flower and bent down to meet her.

"Hide me!" cried Shell-Flower. She ran behind her mother. When the men came even closer, Shell-Flower peeked out. "The owls!" she cried.

Both Grandfather and the white men laughed. The strangers were kind and gentle.

Still, that night, Shell-Flower lay awake, seeing owl eyes everywhere.

The families soon stopped outside of one of the strangers' towns. Grandfather took Shell-Flower's brothers and older sister with him. They came back with wonderful stories of red stone houses and whistling steamboats.

Shell-Flower's brothers had met the strangers. They had not been afraid. Nothing bad had happened.

"Perhaps Grandfather's words are right," Shell-Flower thought.

One day, Shell-Flower's brother brought a new food for her to try. It was from the strangers. They called it *cake*. The taste was so sweet that Shell-Flower could not stop eating it. She had never had anything quite like it.

The next day Shell-Flower was sick.

Mother looked at Shell-Flower's swollen face and touched her hot skin. She held Shell-Flower close as she spoke to Grandfather. "Your white brothers gave us food that made my daughter sick," she said.

Shell-Flower could not open her eyes. She heard her grandfather speak to her mother. "I do not think that the cake has harmed her," he said. "I have eaten it, and so have you. No one else is sick."

Shell-Flower's sickness lasted many days.

As she lay with her eyes swollen shut, she heard a soft voice. She felt gentle hands on her face. She remembered what her father had once told her. He had said that a visitor from the Spirit World comes to watch over a sick person. "The voice must be here to take me to the Spirit World," Shell-Flower thought.

21

The voice said, *"Poor little girl, it is too bad."*

Shell-Flower did not know the meaning, but the sound was comforting. She heard it again and again. *"Poor little girl, it is too bad."* Each time, she felt something touching her face.

At last, Shell-Flower began to feel better. She was able to open her eyes. "Someone from the Spirit World sang to me," Shell-Flower said to her mother and grandfather. She told them about the soft voice and the strange words.

"That voice was not from the Spirit World," said Grandfather. "It was the voice of a good white woman who came to care for you. She put some medicine on your face and spoke kind words to you."

Then Shell-Flower heard the voice again. But this time, the words were different.

"You gave your family quite a scare," said the voice. "That poison oak nearly killed you."

Shell-Flower turned to see the smile of the woman who had cared for her. The woman bent down and placed a gentle hand on Shell-Flower's face.

Shell-Flower stared up at the woman's face without speaking. It was not the face of an owl. It seemed kind and beautiful. It was like the face of a sister.

It was the face of a friend.

Several years later, Shell-Flower went to live among white people. She learned to speak, read, and write English. She took an English name: Sarah Winnemucca.

Sarah learned about the ways of white people. She understood that some white people were kind and could be trusted, just as Grandfather had taught. Others were cruel and could not be trusted.

The Northern Paiute suffered as white settlements grew. Sarah Winnemucca tried to do what was best for her people. She spent her life speaking out for fairness, truth, and peace for the Paiute.

Responding

Think About the Selection

1. How does Grandfather act when he hears of the white people's arrival?

2. How does Shell-Flower feel when she cries out, "The owls!"

3. How does Shell-Flower feel about the woman at the end of the story?
Why do you think this?

Use Clues — Draw Conclusions

Copy the chart. Then add one conclusion for the second set of details.

Clues from the Story	Conclusions
1. News arrives that white people are coming. 2. People in Shell-Flower's camp run to hide.	The Paiute people are afraid of the white people.
1. Shell-Flower eats the cake. 2. She gets sick. 3. Her father and mother eat the cake and are not sick.	?

JOURNEY TO A FREE TOWN

BY DELORES LOWE FRIEDMAN
ILLUSTRATED BY CEDRIC LUCAS

Strategy Focus

Will Jake and his family make it to "true freedom" in Kansas? As you read, think of **questions** about the story that you will want to answer by the end.

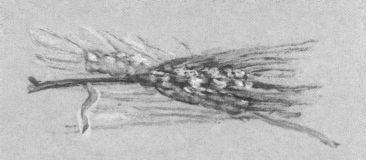

The Civil War was over. People who once were slaves were now free. However, many of these former slaves were now farming land owned by white men. The farmers had to pay the landowners for rent, seeds, and other goods. Although they were not slaves, they still were not truly free.

Some of the farmers, however, escaped and formed new, independent towns in the West. These towns were also called "free towns." Kansas was one state where these towns were started. This is the story of a family's journey to Kansas — and to true freedom.

"Giddyap," Jake yelled, and his old mare looked back. Jake and his son, Matthew, were taking a trip into town.

Jake had been farming cotton in Murfreesboro, Tennessee, for two years, ever since the Civil War had ended in 1865. Every year, he went to town to sell his harvest.

Once he and Matthew arrived in town, they went into Jonah Hopler's general store. Jonah Hopler also owned the land that Jake farmed.

"Morning, Jake," said the man behind the counter.

"Morning, Mr. Hopler. I have this year's cotton crop in the wagon. I'd like to have you price it for me."

Mr. Hopler looked outside and said, "You and your family must've worked pretty hard to get that many bales of cotton in, Jake. Let me just get my book."

Jake didn't have much cash. He had to buy everything — food, clothes, and more — from Hopler. He always paid for it with the money he earned from his crop. Most of the time, Jake left the store still owing Hopler money. This time, however, Jake was sure his crop was so fine he'd be able to sell it, pay the rent, pay for supplies, and still have extra cash to take home.

"I need some seed for beans, some seed potatoes, and a couple of pounds of corn meal," said Jake. "That ought to do it for today."

Hopler wrote in his book and figured numbers for a long time. Hopler always kept more than careful track of everything Jake owed.

"Jake, you've done real good. You made almost enough to pay what you owe on the land. But you know I had to raise the price this year on the seed. So you owe me three and a half dollars and a few pennies. I'll add the seed and meal. Let's just call it four dollars even," he said with a smile.

Jake's jaw dropped open.

"I don't understand this!" he cried. "I worked hard for that money, all year long!"

"I know it's hard for you to understand, but things cost me, so I've got to charge you," said Hopler.

"I understand one thing. I should have some money left over from all that cotton," said Jake. "I came here because I heard you were fair in paying. Maybe I should find a different piece of land to work."

Hopler scowled, "You better not even think of it, Jake. Now, I know how it is, having nothing to show for all that work. I'm going to loan you a half a dollar so you go home with some money in your pocket."

Matthew noticed a stranger who had been standing in a corner of the store. The man was now listening very closely to the argument. Matthew had never seen him before.

Hopler handed some coins to Jake, saying, "I do the same for you as I do for the other folks that work my land."

Jake took the money without saying a word and started to leave.

"Now, don't let me hear your're planning to farm anywhere but my land next year, Jake. If you leave, I'll come looking for you . . ."

Hopler said his parting words to Jake's back as the farmer walked out the door.

As Jake and Matthew walked toward the wagon, the man they had seen earlier quickly walked out of the store and came over to them. He looked serious.

The man handed Jake a small, folded-up piece of paper. "Put this in your pocket," he whispered. He then walked away quickly.

Matthew wondered what was on the piece of paper. They climbed into the wagon and drove home. Jake said nothing all the way there.

At home, Jake told his wife, Doris, what had happened. Doris read the paper out loud:

Ho for Kansas!
New beautiful territory!
Rich soil for farming!
Own your own land!

I feel thankful to inform you that the Real Estate and Homestead Association Will leave here the first day of September, 1868.

For full information inquire of Benj. Singleton, better known as Old Pap, No. 5 North Front Street, Nashville.

Beware of Speculators and Adventurers!

"What do you think, Doris?" Jake asked.

"I think we'll always get cheated if we stay here," she said sadly. "I think we should take to the woods — tonight."

"You sure about this?" Jake asked. "Once we take off, we can't come back. It won't be safe for us. . . ."

"I'm sure," Doris said. "The first thing we need to do is pack our food. Then we pack tools for our crops, and for your blacksmithing. Matthew, you help Pa. Lila, you gather up the food I canned for the winter. We leave after the moon comes up. Like the paper says, Ho for Kansas!"

They took all of their pots, even the big cooking kettle. Jake's wooden plow, along with his hoe, shovel, ax, and tools, went into the wagon too. The last thing they packed was a sack of grain. That was all they had.

"We have to leave as soon as we can get ourselves ready," Jake said. "I don't want anyone to know we're gone until we're long gone. Word might get out to Hopler too soon. "

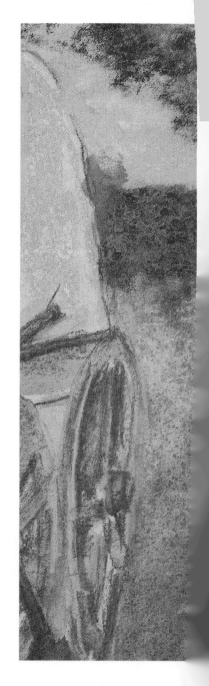

Later that night, they set out.

The back roads were narrow and full of rocks and tree roots. Jake looked at the stars and pointed out the North Star for Matthew.

Every night, they slept on the ground. Soon Matthew lost track of how many days they had traveled. Before dawn one morning, they reached Nashville, Tennessee.

Jake told Matthew to stay put with his mother and sister while he walked into town to find the man named in the poster, Pap Singleton. When Jake came back, he said, "Folks are meeting upriver at the landing."

Many people were waiting at the landing. They carried their belongings in sacks. They were clustered around a tall, gentle-looking man with silver hair. Many boats, following along the riverbank, passed them by. Finally, one stopped. It was a huge steamboat with paddlewheels on either side of it. Tall chimneys on its deck sent out clouds of black smoke. Matthew was excited. This was the boat that would take them to Kansas!

After Pap talked to the captain and handed him some money, the travelers got on the boat.

Matthew couldn't sleep a wink the whole night through. All he could think about was the trip ahead.

The next morning, Pap told Matthew, Lila, and their mother that they would have to get off the boat before it got to St. Louis. The captain said the river up ahead was dangerous, and he wanted to keep the women and children safe.

"Just follow the river, but walk inland," Jake said. "We'll meet you up ahead. By then, we'll be traveling in new wagons that Pap's getting for us."

All the women and children left the boat and started into the woods. A couple of Pap's men went to guide them.

At first, Matthew couldn't see the sky for all the branches in the way. And then, the longer they walked, the fewer trees he saw. They were crossing into the prairie.

Finally, one bright morning, the women and children met up with Jake and the other men. The men were driving six wagons pulled by mules. Lila and the younger children climbed into a wagon. Doris, Jake, and Matthew walked beside them. The group stopped at a creek, filled their water bags, and rested a while. Before long, the journey began again.

One afternoon, Jake and his family stopped at a sign nailed to a tree. In big red letters, it said, "BEWARE OF INDIANS." As Doris read the words to Jake, Pap came up beside them, shaking his head at the sign.

"Don't believe everything you read," Pap said. "Sometimes the Indians are real helpful to us."

They kept walking. Matthew looked around him once or twice, thinking he might see something passing through the darkness.

After many days, they came to a steep riverbank. The men and women had to work together to push each wagon up. Finally, they were worn out. They could not move the last wagon. While they were resting, they heard horses behind them. They turned and saw six Indians, calmly watching them.

Matthew froze. What if the Indians attacked? But Pap had no fear. He walked right up to them with a big smile. He talked to them for several minutes in their language. Before they knew it, the Indians had tied pieces of hide to the last wagon, and their horses pulled it up the riverbank. Pap waved thanks as the Indians rode away.

Matthew looked out on the prairie. He saw only
grass and some bare trees near the riverbank. They set
up a campfire. Everyone listened to Pap talk about
Kansas.

"We've still got quite a ways to go," he said.
"When we get there, we'll have to make dugouts. No
time to build real houses before winter sets in."

"What's a dugout?" Matthew asked.

"It's a hole in the ground we can use as our home,"
said Jake. "You'll see."

Pap asked people what work they did. Jake said he had done some blacksmithing. Jake mentioned that Doris could read. Pap smiled and said, "Well, we've got us a teacher too. Are any of you carpenters?"

A couple of young men in the group raised their hands.

"Good gracious, what a fine town you're going to build!" said Pap. As the campfire crackled, other people piped up. One man said he was a doctor. Another knew how to craft leather. All the people would get to use their skills in their brand-new town.

One day, when the travelers didn't think they could go any farther, the people in front stopped and pointed up ahead.

"We're in Kansas!" they cried.

In the distance, Matthew saw smoke rising out of small houses. They looked as if they were made of mud.

"Pa, that doesn't look like much," Matthew said.

His mother said, "Don't you worry what it looks like."

Jake added, "We're going to build a free town now. It looks real good to me!"

Everyone smiled. It was time to begin a new life.

Responding

THINK ABOUT THE SELECTION

1. Why does the author say that the former slaves are not truly free?

2. Why does the man in Hopler's store wait until Jake and Matthew are outside before approaching them?

3. Why is the sign "BEWARE OF INDIANS" an example of propaganda?

IT'S PROPAGANDA

Copy this chart. Then add two details from the advertisement on page 35 that are examples of propaganda.

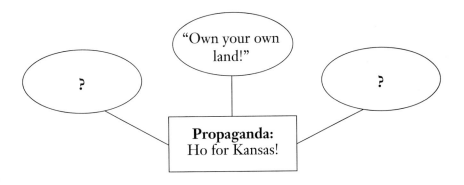

"Own your own land!"

?

?

Propaganda:
Ho for Kansas!

Zachary's Ride

by Chenille Evans
illustrated by Beth Peck

Strategy Focus

Can eleven-year-old Zachary do a man's job? As you read, stop now and then to **evaluate** how Zack deals with riding for the Pony Express.

It was my day off from doing chores out at the El Dorado Ranch. I was excited about having a full day before me with nothing to do.

It was a beautiful morning. I wandered around Sacramento looking in shop windows and getting the latest news from back east. Out here in California, we were the last folks to get the news. Abraham Lincoln had been elected President! He was a tall, skinny fellow, just like me, except I was only eleven, and he was a full-grown man.

As I walked behind the Pony Express station, I heard whinnying and shouting like I'd never heard before. I ran to see what was going on.

A mustang was snorting and rearing something awful. The stationmaster was trying to calm it down, but he wasn't having much luck. I wondered where the rider was. Then I noticed something, and spoke up.

"Hey, mister, there's blood on this horse," I said, trying to steady the animal.

"Blood? Where?" asked the stationmaster, startled.

I pointed, and he eyed the horse's right side.

"That's blood, all right," he said. A red stream ran down the leather saddlebag on the horse's back and down its dust-coated leg. We looked the horse up and down, but we couldn't find a wound.

"It must be Joe's blood," he mumbled.

He opened the saddlebag. The mail was still inside. The stationmaster breathed a huge sigh of relief.

"Thank goodness the mail's still here," the stationmaster said. "It came nearly 2,000 miles from Missouri at five dollars a letter!"

I nearly fell over.

"FIVE DOLLARS!" I shouted.

The stationmaster shrugged. "It's a high price, no doubt about that. But those folks back east are just lining up to pay it! We get the mail from here to there or there to here in ten days, sometimes more. It always depends on the weather. It's the fastest way to deliver the mail."

I let out a whistle.

"See here, young fella, I can't talk all day. I've got to find someone to take this mail to the next relay point," said the stationmaster. "I think Bill's got a pony rider there who can get to the station after that."

My heart started beating fast. "I'll do it!" I shouted. "I can ride as good as anyone in these parts. Better, even."

The stationmaster took a good long look at me.

"I won't let you down. I promise," I said.

"You got a name, son?" he asked.

"Zachary," I answered. "But folks call me Zack."

"How old are you?" he asked.

"Old," I said. "Old enough."

"You got family?" was the next question.

"Back east. I've been on my own since I was nine," I answered. It was the truth. I'd been hired as a cabin boy on a ship out of New York. I jumped ship in California and never looked back.

"Then get going," said the stationmaster. "There's a fresh horse tied up by the stable. You've got one hour to get to the relay cabin, you hear?"

I ran to the horse and swung quickly into the saddle. The stationmaster adjusted the stirrups. He checked the saddlebag filled with mail going east to St. Joseph. It was in order. "It's ten miles out of town," said the stationmaster. "The horse knows the way." Then he added, "I hope."

I was off like a shot. I had no idea where the relay cabin was, but I trusted the horse. After all, Joe's mustang had known the way here.

I rode at full gallop. I wasn't sure the horse
could keep up this pace the whole way, but I had
to get off to a good start. After about ten minutes,
my legs started getting sore. I've always been as
skinny as a rail, just the sort of rider the Pony
Express liked to hire. I didn't have any extra
padding to make my ride easier. I slowed the
horse to a more reasonable speed, and I felt
much better.

Suddenly, I realized I was in the middle of nowhere. There was nowhere all around. Nowhere as far as the eye could see. There were some trees in the distance, but there was no sign that anyone had ever passed through here before.

It made me start to wonder what had happened to Joe. I hadn't given it much thought until now. Had he been attacked by a wild animal? Or had he been shot by an arrow? Or worse?

I was really alone out there. No one would hear me if I screamed. No one would see me if I were attacked. No one would help me if I were in trouble. All sorts of dangers might be lurking behind the trees and around the corners.

Suddenly, the shadows seemed to have eyes. Was there someone following me? I kept thinking another horse was clip-clopping behind me. I kept going. Did I hear that clip-clop sound again? I spun around. Nothing there. So I rode on and tried not to let my imagination get the best of me.

My throat was parched. I went to grab my canteen but I must have left it at the station in all the excitement. Why didn't I check before I left? What would I do without water? Would I die of thirst?

Would I die of hunger too? Of course, I hadn't brought any food with me. A fellow doesn't just carry food around with him wherever he goes, unless he thinks he'll need it.

"I didn't think this one out straight," I said to myself.

My mind began to fill with visions of my own death. I had thought I would live to see my twelfth birthday, but now I wasn't so sure. I began to think this ride wasn't such a good idea.

Suddenly the wind picked up and the sky grew black. A crack of lightning ripped across the sky and split a full-grown tree in the trail just ahead of me. The horse reared up. I tried to hold on but I flipped backwards off the horse and into the dust.

I hit the ground so hard it knocked the wind out of me. I saw stars dancing in my head.

The dust I was lying in didn't stay dust for too long. The sky opened up and the rain poured down like a waterfall. I picked myself up and ran after the horse that was jumping around a little way down the trail.

Mud oozed in through holes in the soles of my boots. I slipped and slid all over the place, trying to get hold of the horse and calm him down.

When I finally got back on the horse, I was soaked to the skin.

I had already worried about dying of thirst. Now I was fretting about dying from the damp. I had no coat, no hat, not even a decent pair of boots to cover my feet. What had I been thinking?

I rode on, but the rain didn't let up. I was grateful that the horse seemed to know where it was going. I couldn't see two feet in front of my face.

Then matters went from bad to worse. Something hit me on the head.

"Ouch!" I shouted. Whatever it was left my head hurting as if I'd been stung by a bee.

It happened again. This time I found the thing that had done it still clinging to my drenched hair. It was a small piece of ice.

Hail.

The hail pelted us. I lunged forward to keep the hail off my face and grabbed the horse around the neck. A hundred ice pellets bounced off my back.

The horse was afraid. So was I. I talked to him.

"It'll be all right, old boy. It'll be all right," I repeated over and over again.

I hoped I was speaking truth.

I rode on, clinging to the horse. I tried not to think about anything other than the rhythm of his hooves and my own breathing.

I started to think in spite of myself. I remembered my family back east. I wished I had never gotten on that ship. I wished I hadn't run away. I wished I had never seen California. I wished I had a warm meal and a dry bed. I wished I had a hat. I wished a lot of things.

The hail let up. Then the rain lessened. The horse and I were exhausted. He whinnied as we went around a bend. I guessed that we were nearing the relay point. I soon saw a cabin about half a mile ahead.

A man with a long yellow coat grabbed the horse's bridle when we rode up to the station.

"Where's Joe?" he asked.

"Missing," I said.

"Well, boy," he said to me, "you're late." He pointed to a fresh horse, as if I were supposed to climb on that one and keep going. "You'll have to do better on the next stretch," he told me.

"Look, mister," I said. "This isn't my job. I did this for fun." I explained what had happened in Sacramento.

"Caleb!" the man called to a boy in the cabin. "How soon can you be ready to ride?"

Two minutes later, Caleb and the horse were disappearing in the distance.

The man looked at me. "What's your name, son?" he asked.

I told him, and he said, "Well, Zack, you still have to do better next time if you want the job."

When he saw my surprised look, the man said, "You've got a job if you want one. The run is 75 miles east one day, 75 miles west the next. You change horses every ten miles or so. Think you can handle that?"

"Will you give me a hat and a coat?" I asked.

"Nope!" the man answered. "But I'll pay you enough to buy one."

"Pay?" I asked.

"A hundred dollars a month," said the man.

My eyes nearly popped out of my head. I worked the figures in my head. That was twenty times what they paid me at the ranch. Plus, they'd never miss me. "You've got a deal!" I shouted.

"You're hired," said the man. "Now get inside. There's a fire and a bed and some hot grub. Eat up and rest. You've got a long way to go in the morning." He pointed east.

I went inside, warmed up in front of the fire, and had some stew. When I was done, I fell into bed. Before long, I was fast asleep, dreaming of my new life with the Pony Express.

Responding

Think About the Selection

1. Why does Zack offer to take the mail?

2. What does Zack mean when he thinks "I didn't think this one out straight"?

3. How do you feel about Zack's leaving his home back east all by himself?

Making Judgments

Copy this chart on a piece of paper. Then complete it to show a judgment you made about Zack. Use this type of chart to make more judgments about Zack.

What the Character Does	What I Think About It	Why I Think This
The stationmaster lets Zack ride to St. Joseph.	The stationmaster should not let a young boy do this.	The ride is dangerous. An adult shouldn't have a boy do this.
Zack decides to make the ride without thinking.	?	?

AMERICA:
A Dream

by Stanford Makishi
illustrated by José Miralles

Strategy Focus

Jiro Akamine came to America with a big
dream. As you read, stop every now and then
to **summarize** each part of the story.

In the late 1800s, people from all over the world were coming to California. They all had a dream of a better life in America. Some of these people, mostly men, came from Japan. This story is about one man, Jiro Akamine. His story is made up from the true stories of many different Japanese men. If Akamine had really lived, he would have told this story when he was a very old man in the 1960s.

My family in Japan did not have much money, but we were happy. Our small farm gave us enough to eat. I had many friends. Most of all, I was proud to work with my mother and father on the farm.

As I got older, though, I wanted more for my family. I thought that if I could get an education, I might be able to have a good job someday.

By the time I turned 14, I knew that I would not get the education that I wanted if I stayed in Niigata. I had a cousin and some friends who had gone to find jobs and go to school in California in America.

I made my decision. I would go to America too.

I came to America with one big dream. My dream was to have a good education. No one in my family had finished school, and I wanted to be the first to do it.

Like some other Japanese people who came to America, my plan was to learn to speak English. I wanted to finish school in America and then go back to Japan. Then, I thought, I could find a good job in my homeland. I was not the only one with this dream.

I came to California in 1885. I had been on a boat from Japan for days and days. Here I was, finally, in San Francisco.

When I walked off the boat, I realized that I would not return to Japan for a very, very long time. I thought about my family in Niigata. For a moment, I had the terrible thought that I might never return to them.

I didn't really know where to go. But that night, I found my way to a rooming house on Golden Gate Avenue. One of my cousins had told me I might rent a cheap room there.

"Hello, my name is Jiro Akamine," I said to the large man in charge. "I would like to rent a room here." I checked the American coins in my hand. My cousin had sent them to me in Japan. "I have only sixty cents," I said.

Luckily, the large man spoke Japanese. He answered, "We rent rooms for fifteen cents per night. Meals are thirty cents per day."

75

I thought for a while. I figured out that I could stay there for four nights with the money I had, if I did not pay for meals. I finally said, "Yes, I would like to rent a room for four nights."

"Okay," the man said. "That will be sixty cents, please." I gave him all the money I had.

"Let me show you to your room," the man said with a kind smile.

As we walked up a flight of stairs and then down a dark hallway, I thought about what I had done. I had a place to stay for four nights, but I didn't know how I would eat. I was scared.

I wondered if I had made a mistake in coming to America. I had no money now, and of course I didn't have a job. I spoke only Japanese. When I arrived, very few people in San Francisco spoke Japanese.

Now I was all alone in a small, dark room.
I did not know what to do. I was very tired,
though, so I just went to sleep.

In the beginning, I could not find work. I found my friends from Japan and borrowed money from them. That way, I could buy food and stay at the rooming house on Golden Gate Avenue. I knew that I had to find a job quickly.

Most of all, I had to stick to my dream of going to school.

After a few hard weeks, I found a job cleaning windows. I slowly started to pay back my friends. Then, at last, I began to study English. I had been in America for nearly two years.

The English lessons were very difficult for me. I had to learn the alphabet, which looked nothing like Japanese writing. And the sounds were very different. I could not always say the words that the teacher taught me.

I studied hard because I had to learn some English before I could get more of an education.

Some people who came with me from Japan worked on farms. Others washed dishes, cleaned streets, or worked as delivery people. Whatever we did, we worked hard, and we took whatever pay we could get. Finding a job was not easy for someone who didn't speak English. But we kept trying, because we believed our dreams might come true in America.

After six months, the lessons took hold, and I learned a little English. After that, I was able to get a better job. My new job was cooking and cleaning house for an American family named Harris. I was also able to start school. I moved to another rooming house so that I could be close to the school and my new job.

The Harrises paid me about three dollars a week. In the morning, I made breakfast and cleaned the kitchen. At first, I didn't know what to do in an American house. All I had ever used for eating were chopsticks. The Harrises' forks, knives, and spoons confused me. It took me a while to understand American customs.

After working for the Harrises for six months,
I was finally able to start making my dream
come true.

In the afternoons, I went to school.

After school, I went back to the Harris
household to make dinner and do more cleaning.
Sometimes, the Harrises sent me home with left-
overs. When they didn't, I usually had to skip
dinner. On those nights, I just went back to my
rooming house on Market Street and slept in my
lonely room, hungry. I wondered more and more
if I should have ever left Japan.

One evening, I just sat in bed after a long day. I was tired and hungry. I had saved about six dollars in two years. My English still was not very good. I wanted to go back to Japan. But I would be ashamed to return without doing what I had come to America to do.

When I thought about my life in Niigata, though, I knew I had no chance of getting a good education there. I would be stuck on my family's little farm for the rest of my life if I went back.

Of course, compared with some of my friends' lives, my life wasn't so bad. One friend, who worked on a farm in Fresno, died from hunger and sickness. Another friend delivered the Japanese newspaper in San Francisco, but he had to live at the newspaper office and he didn't get paid. At least my job was safe and the Harris family was kind to me. I decided to stay a little longer.

The Harrises helped me with my studies whenever they could. My English improved. And I was enjoying school.

By 1900, wonderful, new things were starting to happen. I was able to get a job as a cook and waiter in a restaurant for ten dollars a week. That year, I also met a woman from Japan named Shizuko, who became my wife.

As it turned out, Shizuko and I moved into the Harrises' house. She cooked and cleaned so that we could live there for free. The Harrises were very kind to her too.

Shizuko and I had three children. As they grew older, Shizuko and I decided to move to an apartment of our own. We said a sad good-bye to the Harrises. "You are like a son to me," Mr. Harris said as I shook his hand. "Good luck to you and your family."

On that last day with the Harrises, I think we all wanted to cry.

Even though we stayed in California, Shizuko and I were not American citizens. Back in our day, it was against the United States law for a Japanese person to become a citizen. But our children were American citizens because they had been born here. Our children all went to school. Their English was excellent.

Over the years, I never made it back to Japan.
Shizuko and I raised our family in California when
very few Japanese people lived here. During this
time, it was often hard to be Japanese in America.
We heard stories about fighting between some
Americans and people from Japan. There were
times when people died in these fights.

However, our family was able to stay safe
from this fighting. Shizuko and I were thankful
for this, and we did everything we could to make
sure that our children had good lives.

Sometimes, I wonder what my life would have been like if I had never left Japan. I imagine I would have worked on my family's farm. Life there would have not been so bad, I suppose.

There were times when I have felt like a failure because I never returned to my family in Niigata. Although I learned to speak English pretty well, I never finished school.

When I think about my life in California, though, I realize that perhaps it is better that I did not go back to Japan. Parts of my dream did come true. I did go to school for a time. I found some good jobs. My children got the education I wanted them to have. Even when bad times later came for the Japanese in America, I knew we were here to stay.

When I was a boy, Japanese people came to America hoping for a better life than we had in our homeland. We all worked very hard. I was luckier than some of the others.

As I write this, I am an old man.

It all happened a long, long time ago. But I still remember when America was only a dream for me.

Responding

Think About the Selection

1. What is Jiro Akamine's dream?

2. Akamine sometimes thinks he was a failure. Do you think he was? Why or why not?

3. In one sentence, tell what you think this story was about.

Story Structure/Summarizing

Copy this map. Complete it by adding the setting, main character, problem, and resolution.

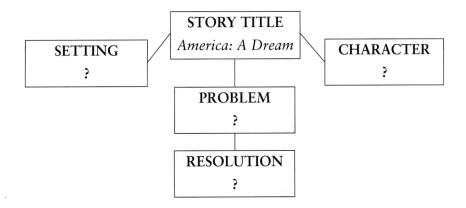

SETTING	STORY TITLE	CHARACTER
?	*America: A Dream*	?

PROBLEM
?

RESOLUTION
?